PEARLS OF WISDOM

"SELF AND OTHER"

EVERYDAY SAYINGS TO ENHANCE YOUR LIFE
BOOK TWO

TRACEY NAVRIDES, MA, LMFT

PEARLS OF WISDOM PUBLICATIONS

This book is dedicated to my mother!
My first "other"!

CONTENTS

INTRODUCTION

I, OTHER & THE RELATIONSHIP

As a psychotherapist, my main goal is to assist people in having healthy relationships. The emphasis of my Master's degree beyond psychology is "the enhancement of intrapersonal and interpersonal relationships". Intra meaning relationship to self which is Pearls of Wisdom, Book 1, *Self and Self*. Inter meaning relationship to other which is this book, Pearls of Wisdom, Book 2, *Self and Other*.

I remind clients often within their primary relationships (significant other, parents, siblings, close friends) there are three components to that relationship: them (the "I"), the other person (the "other") and the actual relationship between the "I" and "other".

In fact, sometimes when I work with a couple, parent/child, or siblings…I will tell them my client is really their relationship not them. My job is to assist the people in my office to have the healthiest relationship possible.

When you think of your relationships, try to remember the existence of the third entity. When you want to "word vomit" all over your "other" try to think about how harmful those words could be to the "other" but also the possible lasting damage you may cause to your relationship.

People forgive each other all the time for harsh words and deeds. Your relationship will never forget and the erosion that occurs each time one or both parties do harm will eventually leave a lasting impression. In the end, both people will remain, but the relationship will be gone. Poof! No more!

How many times have we sat with a friend listening to them tell us they just don't understand what happened to their relationship? They don't even recognize their relationship and nothing feels familiar or safe anymore. Ever been there?

So, try to begin to see all three entities. Try to be mindful and have integrity when approaching your "I", the "other" and the relationship. I realize sometimes people can feel very angry and not respected in their relationships. Try to get beneath the anger (see *The Angry Iceberg* video on my YouTube channel) and figure out how you really feel. This may make you feel vulnerable. Try and come from that place. Your "I", the "other" and your relationship will be healthier because you chose to dig deeper and risk more!

As in Pearls, Book 1 remember these are concepts. Applying them to your life might take a moment and some practice. Some chapters are labeled as ***suggestions*** for how you might shift your perspectives and behaviors, some are ***warnings*** about perspectives and behaviors that might not be serving you and some are both. All are written using Existential Theory....meaning we humans were given *free will* with the *freedom of choice* and the *responsibility for those choices.* The goal is to be respectful and kind to both self, other and the relationship!

I hope this book helps!

DO ONTO OTHERS AS YOU WOULD HAVE THEM DO ONTO YOU

WARNING/SUGGESTION

Boundaries work in both directions. They are a *way of living* for this psychotherapist. Every book I have written and every video I have produced emphasizes boundaries.

For example, it is important I keep my boundaries with my clients. Transference and countertransference is the phenomenon occurring in a therapy session. I have been trained to understand both of these concepts and realize when those boundaries are working in both directions to keep the therapeutic alliance healthy. But my professional alliances are not the focus of this chapter.

The health of a relationship depends on boundaries working in both directions. Are they healthy?

Focusing on healthy boundaries is what I tell clients all the time. I can teach you what a healthy boundary looks like, but ultimately, it is up to you to figure out what those boundaries are in your life. With practice, you can learn how to apply them every day, tweaking the subtle nuances to fit you!

So, with that disclaimer in place, let's see if I can help you figure out first what a healthy boundary looks like and second, why they work in both directions.

I once had someone tell me, "Tracey, no one will ever respect you unless you respect yourself first". Never a truer piece of advice did I get. I was about 31 years old when that advice was given and for the next year or so, I practiced drawing a "respectful" boundary line for myself and in so doing, I figured something out.

I could draw all the respectful, healthy boundary lines I wanted. BUT, ***and this is a big but,*** if I danced across my own boundary line, I was giving permission to the other person to dance across it as well. What do I mean by that?

I will use an age old example of women and men. If a man is interested in you and you are not interested in him, other than as a friend, the logical and respectful thing to do is to tell him, thereby, establishing a boundary of friendship ONLY.

Now, here is the tricky part…how does one define friendship? Ask yourself this question as you read this and write down your response.

My definition of friendship goes as follows: mutual respect for one another's thoughts, feelings, and physical being. Compliments are held to a level standard of kindness, nothing overboard. For example: "You look nice today, have you been working out?" OR "I really like your outfit."

Nothing too over the top! For example: "Wow! You look like a million dollars, my goodness you sure are looking GOOD today. You look so good, I could eat you up!"

Hear the difference? The first examples have a modicum of reserve and respectability, the second examples are over the top and imply more than they should and so on.

Now, here is the challenge for you, reader…if you were the one who set the "just friends" boundary, you cannot dance across that boundary line and make those types of second example compliments. It would give your friend the wrong idea and pretty soon, they will be coming across your boundary thinking it is okay, because you crossed your boundary first. Understand?

Very simple example and I am sure you are applying this idea right now as you think about your life. Yes? Okay, now let's talk about *boundaries work in both directions.* I will use the prior example, then a young adult and parent as my second example.

In the prior example of women and men, now expanding to be all inclusive with those preferring to be known as non-binary...as you were the one who initiated the boundary of "just friends" you need to make sure your friend understands they cannot cross the boundary you have made. This would be what is called an "agreement" between the two of you.

Many theorists in my field talk about how each and every day, we human beings make small and large agreements and every measure in between within our relationships. What keeps a relationship healthy is the integrity within those agreements.

Back to my boundary example...your friend cannot step across your boundary of "just friends" which may sound obvious to you and repetitious on my part. You also cannot step across their boundary of agreeing to your "just friends" status. Right? An agreement goes both ways!

Now let's say you show up one day feeling particularly down about yourself and your life. Accidentally, you make a flirtatious comment to your friend. Your "friend" may decide to cross your boundary because YOU just crossed your boundary!

Maybe you were simply feeling vulnerable that day and needed your friend to help you feel better about yourself. What if on that same day, your friend rebuffs you because they are holding your boundary line, the agreement they made with you, even though you didn't. Once you explain your vulnerability and apologize for crossing your boundary and being wonky on the agreement, the boundary can be drawn again and your friendship will stay intact.

See what I mean about the nuances of boundaries being difficult to grasp sometimes. Let's look at my second example and see if things get a bit clearer.

A young adult, John and his parent, Lucy are having a hard time figuring out the boundaries between them. John is declaring his independence on a daily basis. When faced with real world issues like scheduling his time, eating properly, and getting to work, John is struggling. Within this struggle he continues to seek out Lucy's assistance (i.e., doing his laundry, paying his bills, his meals being prepared, gas in his car, his doctors' appointments being scheduled). One day Lucy makes a comment about time management in an attempt to help John figure out how to handle his daily life with greater ease. John fires back..."It's my life, don't tell me what to do, I will handle it!" Lucy is left feeling used, abused, taken advantage of and is made to feel like the *bad guy.*

Did you suss out the boundary issue? This young adult is declaring they can take care of themselves, then promptly and repeatedly dances across the boundary line. When this parent earns the right (with all the assistance) to step across the **child's** boundary line to give an opinion or advice, the **child** promptly berates the parent, and pushing back across the line, re-declares that it is their life, don't tell them what to do, and they will handle it!

But John isn't handling it and continuously asks his parent for assistance. He danced across his own boundary line of independence/young adulthood and is now punishing his parent for doing the same! Notice I went from describing John as a young adult in the first paragraph to describing him as a **child** in the second paragraph...why? Because that is how he is behaving!

Now, please do not misunderstand me...young adults are learning to take care of themselves. It begins around 14 or 15 and grows from there. This is not an easy transition (see my YouTube Channel and the video *Abstract Thinking*). Let's continue with this example...

Remember, integrity goes both ways. Somewhere in their relationship, both John and Lucy made an agreement and a boundary that he would *run his own life, Lucy would stop telling him what to do, and he would handle it.*

Clearly John is not handling his life, is breaking the agreement and crossing the boundary they made. John's integrity is in jeopardy, however, young adults are learning (prefrontal cortex growth, moral, ethical code, and integrity development until age 26). John is practicing boundary formation.

If these two were my clients, I would encourage Lucy to honor the boundary agreed upon, thereby, modeling integrity and respect for the boundary she and John made.

In Pearls, Book 3 for parents, I write about *"do as I say, not as I do"* which implies a double standard. One standard for the parent and a different standard for the child. When working with teens it becomes about how parents show up and their actions, not what they say to their children. How parents behave needs to be congruent with their words. But that's the parenting book...back to the example!

I would suggest Lucy's behavior look like this...no laundry done, no gas money, no bills paid, no scheduling of doctor's appointments, no meals made, PERIOD! Lucy is honoring the boundary John requested.

Now, John with his boundary in place would have to learn how to handle his life! Hey, what a concept! He would have to figure out how to live with the boundary he made, the agreement that was put in place with his parent. He would have to grow up! And, Lucy would no longer look like the bad guy or feel used and abused. See how the boundaries work in both directions?

Mutual respect and integrity for one's self and others is at the heart of healthy boundaries. Many of my clients when first introduced to these concepts, felt as if boundaries were mean! They are not! People who have learned to create healthy boundaries feel better about themselves and their relationships. They feel respected and understood.

And John...He was asking to feel respected and understood with his newfound boundaries of living his own life (time management, eating well, laundry done, etc). To infantilize him by allowing him to dance across his own boundaries he declared might do him greater harm and keep him small. Much more harm than some dirty clothes or take out food because no dinner was prepared.

By respecting their boundaries, a parent empowers their child allowing them to stand on their own two feet, to make mistakes, to learn and grow. The boundaries work in both directions with each side respecting the other. Within adversity, we humans grow! By allowing their child to figure things out, that parent helps that child mature.

When a parent feels anxiety over watching their child struggle with those boundaries in the example, use empathy...for example: "I can see you are having difficulties. Sometimes, healthy boundaries can be hard. I am really proud of you for wanting to stand on your own two feet!" Got it?

The title of this chapter is *do onto others as you would have them do onto you!* Healthy boundaries are the foundation for this saying as they create a relationship between self and other fostering respect, trust and love!

Next!

MAKE FAIR AGREEMENTS AND STICK WITH THEM (CONFUCIUS) LITTLE AND LARGE AGREEMENTS AND ALL SIZES IN-BETWEEN

SUGGESTION

On the heels of that last chapter as you know, I talk to people all time about *agreements* between them. Inevitably, whenever I am working with clients one of the issues commonly troublesome are *agreements* that have been broken. Whether it is a couple or family members, if one or more people continue to break the *agreements* they have made with one another, the respect and trust breaks as well. Over time, repeating the behavior of broken *agreements* will lead to anger and resentments, sometimes resulting in separation and the end of relationships.

Some examples of *little agreements* might be taking out the trash, cleaning one's room, walking the dog. Some examples of *large agreements* might be maintaining sobriety, not spending too much money, talking the talk and walking the walk!

If all of us maintained our integrity every time we made an *agreement* with someone and followed through with the *agreement* every time...think of how much more fulfilling our lives would be and how much easier it would be to count on one another!

Let me give some real world examples…

He or she who cooks does not clean! So, whoever took the time to cook the meal, the other person or persons does the dishes. If the cook doesn't see the dishes get done in a timely manner after the meal, and this happens too often, the cook won't be inspired to cook anymore. Why would they? The *agreement* keeps getting broken. There is no inspiration within a broken *agreement*!

Chores around the house are assigned to each member of the household. If all members of the household don't accomplish their chores in the agreed upon timeframe, the tension in that household will become unbearable. Members of the household will stop speaking to one another, resentments will be built and everyone will be walking around on eggshells. All this tension could have been completely avoided had everyone simply done their chores agreed upon, in the timely manner also agreed upon. Harmony would reign in this household!

I think you get my gist! I would imagine you are thinking up all kinds of agreements in your own life as you are reading this….so now, let me move on to negotiating those *agreements* as this is an important step in actually achieving them with integrity and consistency.

Do your best not to agree to things simply because you want the person to go away. They are annoying you so telling them what they want to hear, gets them to go away. Or you always agree to everything because you are a people pleaser.

If your motivation does not take into account your desire to accomplish the *agreement,* then you will fail. And guess what? You will lose credibility with the person you have chosen to go into agreement with…how about that?

You may not believe me, but you have the ability to negotiate the *agreement*. So does the other person. For both your sakes, negotiate! Take the time to sit down together and figure out to the best of your abilities, how each of you can get an *agreement* on the table that works for you ***both***. If you succeed at creating an *agreement* that works for you ***both***, the chances of ***both*** of you succeeding in maintaining the *agreement* go up exponentially. There were multiples of ***both*** in those last sentences. Can you guess why??? Go back to Chapter 1!

NOTE: Human beings have the hardest time doing anything consistently. We just do! Maintaining consistency takes mindfulness and effort. So, if you make an *agreement* with someone be it *"little or large"* and it isn't a one time *agreement,* make sure you consistently repeat the behaviors involved with that *agreement* over and over.

NOW, you can renegotiate if an *agreement* stops working for you. Don't just let the original *agreement* fall to the wayside because there goes your credibility to renegotiate!!!! By maintaining your integrity with the original *agreement,* you give yourself the respect and trust along with the other person. You stand on solid ground for your new negotiation!

And remember what Confucius say...*Make Fair Agreements and Stick With Them!*

Win/win for everyone!!!!

HOWEVER HIGH YOUR EXPECTATIONS WILL EQUAL HOW BIG YOUR DISAPPOINTMENTS

WARNING

The problem with *expectations is the higher they are, the bigger our disappointments will be.* This concept includes self expectations and expectations of others. The harder a person is on themselves, the harder they are on others. Sometimes people are not aware of this *expectation.*

They think they give people a "pass" and are really only tough on themselves. Frankly, I don't think this is true. I think people have to admit to themselves and their loved ones that they are equally tough on self and others. Only then, can they begin to manage their *expectations.*

It is very difficult not to expect. We spend years in a relationship only to have it end. We think very highly of our friends and coworkers, only to be disappointed by their behaviors. We dedicate ourselves to our career, only to feel a lack of fulfillment. We go on vacation, we expect to have a good time. We buy something, we expect it to measure up to our investment. Speaking of investments, we expect the market to do well and not plummet, losing everything. We expect a lot from people, situations, places and circumstances.

How do we manage our *expectations* so our *disappointments* don't rule us? You already know what I am going to say! Think about your view and what you have control over (existentialism at it's best, free will and all). See if you can put into perspective on a scale of 1 to 10, what your *expectation* may be. Try and temper that *expectation* based on the following: can't control the weather on a vacation, can't necessarily control a product's viability (see if it is returnable), can't control the stock market, can't control other human beings and remember we are all imperfect. Once you begin to understand all of that, then you can manage your *expectations,* thereby, lowering the number of *disappointments* in your life.

One more thing...remember that YOU are an imperfect human being as well. If you are putting out into the world your high *expectations,* others are most likely viewing you with their own measure of high *expectations* on you! Be careful not to hold others to an *expectation* you yourself would not live up to. We all get to be human!

However,

There are those people who hold others to a higher *expectation* than they do themselves. These are the people who have a "double standard". They expect more from everyone, but don't ask the same of themselves, then wonder why people build resentments against them. In other words, they need to look in the mirror!

Here is a real world example:

Jenny was a single mom of two girls. She was always relying on her ex-spouse, Rick to take the girls to doctors' appointments, game practices, etc. If he ever said no because of a scheduling conflict, she would become very upset and angry with him. She even accused him of being a "bad father" when he was unavailable to help.

Meanwhile, she rarely helped him when needed, so he stopped asking and learned he couldn't count on her.

One day, Rick really needed her to handle a doctor's appointment for one of their daughters. It had been scheduled months in advance, but he had a work related conflict and was stuck. She agreed to take their daughter, then forgot the appointment and didn't show.

When confronted with the missed appointment, Jenny acted as if it was no big deal and wondered why Rick was so upset. Rick tried to explain to Jenny how often he is expected to take the girls. The one time he asked her to help him, she didn't come through. She refused to apologize or even admit she did anything wrong! This is an example of a "double standard".

These types of people are hard to deal with because they expect much and give little! Measuring one's *expectations* with someone like this would be important in order to keep your *disappointments* to a minimum. Although these people exist in the world, it is important for you to keep your perspective healthy and behave accordingly.

That's why I always ask...what do YOU have control over? You have control over ***your view*** and ***your actions***. Your *expectations* should align with your self integrity, thereby, integrity for others. Make sure you don't *disappoint* yourself or others too often!

YOU CAN MEASURE A PERSON'S INSANITY BY HOW MANY MAYBES THEY HAVE IN THEIR LIFE

WARNING/SUGGESTION

I love this saying! Why? It speaks to the struggles we humans have with ambiguity. We don't do well with the *gray* area. It would be much easier for us if everything were *black or white*. The minute there is more than one way or the other, we become very uncomfortable. So, what is the answer? The answer is to make sure that one doesn't have too many *maybes* in their life at the same time....let me explain.

Maybes equal *ambiguity*. One of the definitions of *ambiguity* is *uncertainty*. If there is too much *uncertainty* in a person's life, anxiety will be the result. Create enough anxiety in a person's life and a measure of *insanity* will occur.

The reason why I included this chapter in this book of *self and other* (just as easily could have been included in the Pearls, Book 1) is because often times ambiguity is created by others in our lives, by circumstances that might be beyond our control and it is up to us to manage the *maybes*.

So, how do we do that? The first thing to ask ourselves is "what am I in control of?" You are certainly in control of your view of a situation and how you respond to it. A lot of us forget this, but remember I am a Humanistic Existential psychotherapist. I feel for your struggles with my whole heart being a human myself. I am going to ask you to exercise your free will and remember that you have more power than you think. You have power over yourself and how you behave, react and choose to be.

Using a real world example...

Judy's life seemed to be falling apart. Her job was experiencing layoffs and she was not sure if she would be let go. Her relationship was having difficulties and she and her partner didn't seem to be communicating anymore. Both Judy's professional and personal life seemed to be in a very *ambiguous* place. There is that word again. In other words, she had some pretty serious *maybes* in her life. Did I mention she was worried about her health?

Judy came to see me with these issues. I don't know if I have said this previously, but it takes much courage and bravery to seek therapy. This is not an easy feat! I give a lot of kudos to my clients or any person that makes it into therapy. I digressed...

So, Judy came into my office looking to lower her anxiety over all of these *maybes*. You already know what I asked her after she told me what was going on.

I asked her what does she have control over? Once she figured that out, I asked her what direction she might want to pursue?

In the case of her job, could she put some resumes out, ask some friends for opportunities, see what might be available for her to pursue? In the case of her relationship, would couples therapy be an option? If not, what was within her control and how would she like to proceed based on her answers. Regarding her health, did she need to educate herself on what might be going on, get a second opinion, figure out what might be the *root cause* of the issue. Do you see where I am going?

By understanding what she had control over (herself), Judy had the ability to see more than one way to view what was going on in her life. By realizing she had choices, she could go into action, thereby, lowering the *ambiguity* in her life, lowering the *maybes* in her life, lowering the *insanity* in her life. She may not be able to control everything (her job ends?) but by changing her view and going into action, she can feel in control of her destiny. Isn't that what we humans strive for among other things?

Whenever you feel as if you have *too many maybes in your life and your insanity feels too much,* ask yourself "what am I in control of?" Start from there....

MISERY LOVES COMPANY

WARNING/SUGGESTION

We have all met these people! They have been called "Eyeore" after the beloved character in Winnie the Pooh. Always looking at the dark side of every situation. Never seeing the good in anything. Before I continue with this chapter, I want to qualify….I am not writing about those of us who suffer from debilitating anxiety or depression. Those folks have a chemical imbalance in their brain only allowing them to read negativity into their lives and situations. I am addressing the people who use their *misery* to make others around them miserable. After all, *misery loves company!* Having *company* is what they thrive on!

One of the biggest challenges a person could face is having someone they love who chooses to live in *misery*. This person could be a family member, a friend or a significant other. There are ways to live in *misery*. Here are a couple of different perspectives:

As I mentioned at the beginning of this chapter, they see the world from a very Eyeore lens. Eyeore never thought anything was going to go right for him or anyone else. Even if the contrary were to happen and things turned out well, Eyeore would find a way to poke holes in the positive. I remember as a child saying, "we're all doomed"* as a way of expressing something Eyeore might say. However pessimistic Eyeore might have been, he never inflicted his pessimism on others. He went inward with his negativity. *Misery loves company* does not apply to Eyeore!

A more potent perspective of this title is the person who weaponizes their *misery* by claiming they are a victim to everything. Ever met someone like that? They use their victimhood to fail. They constantly claim everyone is against them…their family, their friends, their work, even society. They accuse others of sabotaging them. They can never get ahead because someone or something is keeping them from accomplishing their goals, their dreams, their life.

In reality, they themselves are guilty of their own sabotage. They are in an endless circle of causality where they are the beginning, the middle and the end of creating their own *misery*, their own failures, their own demise. It is hard to watch and be a part of this person's life, especially if they are someone you love and care about!

Here is a benign, yet real world example…

Paul is having a bad day. Pretty much every day is a bad day for Paul because his childhood was traumatic, his adult life is not much better. He has no significant other in his life, he works in a dead end job and pretty much feels miserable all the time. Every person he encounters throughout his day gets his bad, upset, surly mood snapped at them. His family and what few friends he has tend to avoid him because they don't want to become as miserable as him. With each passing day, Paul feels as if no one likes him, everyone hates him and he is simply existing.

If Paul found his way to therapy, any therapist might be

able to assist Paul in understanding that he has created his own reality of *misery*. Oh yes, does his childhood trauma influence him? Absolutely! However, if he gave himself that chance to heal from it and began to see his life through a different lens, maybe his *misery* would subside. Maybe, he would turn his surly mood around, begin to act differently with the people in his life and maybe, people would begin to gravitate towards him rather than away from him!

In the end, if you or someone you know bears witness to a person who makes it their life's mission to make everyone else around them miserable using their own *misery* through guilt, accusations and victimization, please pass this along:

One of the abilities a therapist has to cultivate is the ability to understand that a client's struggle, although hard to witness can create much anxiety within the therapist. The struggle belongs to the client, therefore, must be figured out by the client. The therapist's job is to join them where they are and to keep our anxiety and expectations in check.

A person who finds themselves bearing witness to a loved one's *misery* wants to reach out to provide support and comfort. Sometimes that's about alleviating the anxiety you feel around this very tragic situation, however, although you are allowed to have all of your feelings about this, your loved one has to be as uncomfortable as they make everyone else before they may act to change their situation. You might read that last paragraph again!

Your attempt to help moves their focus off of them and puts it on you, thereby, giving them an "out" as they go after you for being kind. Sitting with your feelings in the latest episode of their *misery* is the cross you have to bear, that all of your family and friends will bear. You are not alone and recognize that although any one of us could be in those shoes, we chose to not be a victim, to have enough integrity

(Respect, Trust, Love (RTL)) for ourselves and others and to become brutally honest to create change in us. Until your family member or friend is willing to do that, *misery loves company* and nothing anyone says or does will make a difference!!!

In review, the aforementioned paragraphs and examples were the **Warning!**

Now let's focus on a **Suggestion!**

Recently, I was in session with a client who gave me a whole different perspective on *misery loves company* that I would like to share with you. I had worked with this client for a bit around a tragedy that occurred in their life and the grief they were experiencing. One of the interventions therapists use to assist a client in session is to "normalize" what a client is going through, thereby, assisting them to understand they are not alone in their human condition. In this particular scenario, it was the grief surrounding the loss of a loved one.

One of the client's responses during our session was, "Well, you know *misery loves company*". I asked for the client to elaborate on what they meant because my understanding of this particular saying was the example I gave earlier in this chapter.

My client went on to tell me that as miserable as they were in their grief, it was comforting to know that others had gone through similar feelings and thoughts which meant they were not alone.

I commented on what a wonderful way to view a saying that historically always meant something negative rather than positive. My client gave me a gift that day and this chapter is dedicated to them!

How powerful our existential view can become if given the chance to be different! I challenge you to choose every day how to change your view towards health and healing. I didn't say it would be easy, but I have faith in you! I know you do, too!!!!

*Please note: Eyeore never said "we're all doomed". You can go onto the internet and get a loose diagnosis of each character of the Winnie the Pooh series which leaves me a bit disturb, truth be told!

NO IS AN OKAY ANSWER!

WARNING/SUGGESTION

You would be shocked at how many of us never learned to accept *"no"*! Conversely, you would be shocked at how many of us never learned to say *"no"*! *No is an okay answer!!!!*

Let me backup for a minute.

We should have learned how to accept *"no"* as an okay answer when we were young. Life is full of limits, full of do's and don'ts. Learning to accept those limits is paramount to us living in a socially acceptable society. But some of us think we are above those limits. The rules don't apply to us. We are free to do whatever we want, whenever we want. For these people the word *"no"* is ***NOT*** an okay answer! You need to watch out for them!

Most of us have struggled with learning and practicing how to say *"no"*. Why? Plain and simple because whenever we say *no* to someone, we feel bad. We worry about disappointing them. We don't want to be the bad guy.

The problem with never saying *no* usually means we overextend ourselves, have really wonky boundaries that everyone dances over showing us a lack of respect for our time, energy and money (three finite resources). We are generally taken advantage of for our kindness.

How do we learn to accept "*no*" and say "*no*"? Well, I believe throughout our lifetime we probably receive as many "*no*s" (plural) as we give. There is balance in that belief. It helps me to believe in that balance. It helps me accept "*no*" when given by another and say "*no*" when needed. Let's examine both of these in greater detail.

Learning to say "*no*" takes practice. For those of us who are people pleasers, this can be very difficult. So here is a tool…when someone comes to you asking for something, if you have a hard time saying "*no*" you could say, "Let me think about it and I will get back to you shortly."

I love this response. Why? It gives you a chance to step away from the immediate pressure of answering your friend, family member, colleague in the moment as they are standing in front of you. It gives you some time and space to really assess whether or not you can give them a "yes" that doesn't take away from your life. It gives you the time to check in with you and ask yourself if you have the time and energy or money to give to their ask. It gives you time to respect and trust yourself within a healthy boundary.

If you decide that "*no*" is your answer you must be willing to live through some discomfort when you tell the other person what you have decided. Remember this…you took the time and energy to really think about whether you could give them "their ask" which shows respect for them. By initially giving respect for yourself and your process, you end up giving respect to them as well.

Now, they may not like your "*no*". After all, remember what I said at the beginning of this chapter…most of us never learned to accept the word "*no.*"

I am going to go in two different directions right now. First direction…I will address what may be your feelings and reactions to someone not accepting your "*no*". Second direction....I will address when someone like yourself feels as if they are stuck whether they say "yes" or "*no*" to someone.

So, the first direction...Often, I tell my clients when you take the time to weigh a decision and choose to say "*no*"...the other person is now standing on the other side of your "*no*" boundary.

NOTE: saying "*no*" is definitely a boundary one has drawn, hopefully, for the good of all.

As I was saying, the person standing on the other side of your "*no*" boundary is within their rights to not like your "*no*"...not appreciate your boundary and as I tell my clients, may jump up and down like a little monkey (I like using this descriptor because little monkeys are cute, my clients won't feel inwardly threatened or intimidated by how upset the other person may become) throwing bananas at you in protest of your "*no*" sometimes whole bushels of bananas based on how intense their displeasure is in your boundary.

By using this metaphor, I help my clients and hopefully, you the reader to understand someone is allowed to feel displeased by your choice and decision. You have the ability to not catch those bananas being thrown at you.

NOTE OF IMPORTANCE: By not catching those bananas, you choose to not "fix" their upset over your "*no*". Not because you don't care and/or love them, but because you do! It is not your job to fix their upset. Now, this might be uncomfortable for you. You may experience all kinds of feelings such as: discomfort, sad, hurt, unkind, mean, to name a few. Be careful not to allow these feelings to change your mind. You were thoughtful in your original decision. Stick by it! If still struggling, here is a tool and a way of viewing it that may help...

You could have empathy for them as they struggle with your "*no*". They are struggling. Very apparent in how many bananas/protests/reasons they are giving you to pressure you into changing your mind. Again, not your job to fix their upset. It is your job to empathize with their upset, understanding that we humans don't really like to be told "*no*". Remember?! I think you've got it!

Onto the second direction…many of us deal with one or more persons in our lives that simply will not take "*no*" as an answer. They work manipulatively with us to get their way, no matter the costs to anyone else. What does that look like?

It might look like someone badgering us until we give in, using guilt and our integrity to get us to change our minds. And often, we will give in, change our minds, thereby, reinforcing their behaviors. They threw enough bushels of bananas at us, we just can't hold our "*no*" with any real strength or conviction!

The problem with going back on our "*no*" is then we feel obligated and forced into accommodating (see my YouTube channel for a video and animated illustration on accommodating in couples and families) our little monkey (again, loose depiction of someone we value, could be someone we look up to, admire, an elder).

The long term issue here is…if we give in constantly to this person we will begin to resent them, we will not enjoy our time with them and may even avoid them when possible. Do you see how not honoring our "*no*" creates massive repercussions over time and could ruin the fabric of a relationship we value? A relationship we hold near and dear to our hearts! Saying "*no*" and creating healthy boundaries within our relationships is extremely important! *No is an okay answer.*

So that is saying "*no*" to someone in the second direction…but as I mentioned earlier, what if you simply can't stand in your "*no*" and you end up saying "yes" every time?

As I wrote, you could develop massive resentments

towards that person, however there is a weird phenomenon that can also occur when you are put in a position where no matter what answer you give, *"yes or no"* you lose! It is called "being stuck between a rock and a hard place". Next chapter!!!

STUCK BETWEEN A ROCK AND A HARD PLACE

WARNING

We have all experienced this! Another way of describing this phenomenon is *"damned if you do, damned if you don't"*. I combined both of these as I think they are highly related and work off one another. So here goes...

Referencing back to the previous chapter about "yes and no" answers to those we love and care for, wanting to take a moment in consideration of the ask, then respond from a healthy, respectful boundary...what if no matter what direction you go in, whether it be "yes" or "no" everyone loses? Let me give a real world example:

Jim has a brother named Jeff who struggles through life. This poor man can't seem to get ahead. One of the reasons is that Jeff never learned how to accept *"no as an okay answer"*. Unfortunately for him, the word "no" is NOT an okay answer. Remember in the previous chapter I mentioned you have to watch out for these people. Here is why...

Whenever Jeff gets in a bind, he calls on his big brother to fix it for him. His asks usually involve having nowhere to stay or to live. He has ended up in Jim's spare room, sometimes for weeks and months at a time. Once even for a whole year Jeff stayed at Jim's vacation cabin. These asks from Jeff to Jim always come with promises of rent to be paid (even a small amount is better than nothing), chores to be done, and handyman work around Jim's house or cabin. Unfortunately, Jeff always drops the ball, leaving Jim feeling betrayed over and over again. One of the by-products is the strain on Jim's marriage and family. At the end of each of these situations, there is a big blowup between the brothers due to Jeff's behaviors and lack of boundaries, leaving them not speaking to one another with hurt feelings on both sides.

Jim came to session to discuss some issues he was needing to work on and his brother Jeff came up in conversation as we were discussing "no is an okay answer".

Jim shared with me how he always feels *stuck between a rock and a hard place* when it comes to saying "no" to his brother because every time he gives in and says "yes" everyone loses. Jim was so upset by the end of his story with his brother, he simply wanted to know from me if it would be okay to disconnect from Jeff completely, severing all ties. What a mess! My heart went out to Jim and Jeff. Neither of them knew how to say the word "no" and accept the word "no".

My job as a psychotherapist is to assist people in learning healthy boundaries. My work was cut out for me in this situation. I was going to try and help Jim see that telling his brother "no" may be uncomfortable for him at first. I suggested he sit down and have a heart to heart discussion with Jeff, sharing with him that by always telling him "yes" was not really helping either of them. Telling Jeff "no" was really difficult for Jim, but for the sake of their brotherly relationship, he was going to need to start saying "no" to him.

As it happened, Jim came to session one day after Jeff came around asking to stay at Jim's while his new apartment was being refurbished. It would only be for a few weeks. Jim chose that moment to have the conversation he and I had talked about in the prior session, outlining healthier boundaries between the two. Jeff behaved, as I warned Jim he might, like the little monkey throwing bushels of bananas at him in protest. Jim held his ground and chose not to catch any of the bananas. He empathized with Jeff's upset, understood this was new territory for them both, but held to his "no".

As happens often when a person draws a boundary with a "no", Jeff stormed off and didn't talk to his brother for months. Jim carried a lot of guilt around their last meeting and there was much discussion in subsequent sessions with me. He knew it was the right choice, saying "no" but the guilt and unfamiliar feelings of a healthy boundary ate at him.

I asked the challenge question, "How many times have you and Jeff ended in an argument when you said yes over and over again?" Jim's response was, "Too many to count." I pointed out that if the outcome will always be upset, isn't it better to choose the healthy boundary, thereby, respecting and caring for you both? Jim agreed.

You see, Jim was *damned if he did and damned if he didn't.* Jeff, along with Jim's help had stuck them both *between a rock and a hard place.*

Jeff is still struggling in the world. Jim shares with me that he feels for his brother, but his brother's issues are not his to solve and enabling him is not helpful. When the family gets together for holidays, they stay respectful of one another to honor the family, but Jim will never let Jeff in close enough again to wreak havoc on either of them. Jim hopes that one day his brother Jeff will as he says, "grow up". That is my hope as well! But, Jeff is not my client and I am very proud of the work Jim has done creating the healthy boundaries that allow him to live with respect, trust and love for self first, then other! Enough said!

USE YOUR WORDS

SUGGESTION

Communication vs. Confrontation! Often times, I sit across from a couple or an individual having difficulty expressing themselves. As I dig deeper and ask them to give me examples of how they express themselves, they exhibit behavior more confrontational, not communicational (there's a word!).

Communication is an art. People who do it well are rare. A wordsmith or a human dictionary are descriptions of those who use language to best express themselves clearly and concisely. It is, as if, they are composing a dance in their heads and mapping out each move. With every word or phrase planned ahead of time in order to get their thoughts and feelings across to the listener, in a way the listener can receive and absorb.

People who are really good communicators take into account whom they are addressing, the mood at the time, the context of what they are trying to say, and the possible outcomes of how the listener may perceive their message. This is where confrontation comes into play.

Confrontation can be a nasty piece of business if done

with knee jerk, hostile intentions. We have all been on the receiving end of hostile confrontation and possibly been guilty of blasting someone with our own hostility. My question to you...did your behavior or the other person's behavior (the one blasting you) get you or them what they want?

Confrontation does not have to be negative, nor have a negative outcome. By using communication, one can achieve one's goals...another question...what is your goal?

Figure out what your goal is first before speaking with someone that you may be upset with, then work backwards to figure out how to communicate your needs without accusing the other person or becoming defensive and nasty to get your point across.

Here is "kind of" an example…

When I sit with a couple and ask what is their goal for coming to therapy, I kid you not, the number one (1) goal of a couple is better communication. Upon further questioning, I find out they are confronting each other rather than communicating with each other.

As the weekly sessions continue, my job is to "triangulate" myself into their dynamics as a couple. By doing so, they allow me to do what is called "reframing". Reframing is where I take their words and communication with one another and apply different verbiage and a different approach they didn't think of because they are within their "system"! Their system is their relationship. Like a "family system" they are a "couple system". When we are part of a system it can be difficult to see things from an objective not subjective view.

I am on the outside of their system. This allows me to see things differently than they do and gives me the opportunity to assist them in changing their way of looking at an issue between them. This helps them shift how they communicate with one another, thereby, bettering their communication!

Their original goal! Now, this takes practice! Much practice!!!

In time, most couples graduate or launch from therapy with new communication tools to assist them for life. A caveat here...they can always come back for a "tune up" with me whenever needed usually due to a new stressor or life issue. But that is another story!

Remember when parents began to teach their young toddler to, *"Use your words"*! It took the toddler a bit of time to learn. That is exactly what I am suggesting here! *Use your words*! And be patient with yourself and other!!!!!! It will take time for you to learn!

BE WARY OF PEOPLE THAT COME BEARING GIFTS!

WARNING

One of the observations I have made over the years while listening to others tell me stories of people they thought were their friends..."when I first met them, they were so nice, when I was in the hospital they came to visit me, they seemed to go out of their way to do nice things for me"...and so on.

We have all heard these stories...however, as time goes by the narrators of these stories began to notice these "friends" that in the beginning seemed "so nice, so kind, so generous" were now, not as nice, not as kind, not so generous! How could that be?

Sometimes it is what I call "Shiny Penny" (see my YouTube channel video of the same name). Briefly, when a friendship or relationship is new, people tend to bring others in too quickly, give too much too soon creating an unhealthy co-dependent boundary issue. What do I mean by that?

We are all raised to be "social beings" in order to get along in society. There are rules of etiquette...how to show up well, how to treat others, how to behave, etc.

One of the problems that arise from being social beings...

where to draw the line, where to draw the boundary regarding how much we do for others. Part of this lesson comes from how we were raised in our Family of Origin (FOO). If our FOO was fairly healthy or "good enough" then we probably have pretty good boundaries. If our FOO was dysfunctional, as is the case most of the time (because human beings are not perfect), then we may be missing some of those healthy boundaries.

If, for instance, we were raised by a parent who made us feel guilty every time they did something nice for us, that would teach us the lesson that "if I do that to others, then they will feel guilty and responsible for my emotional well-being." NOW, this is a very simplistic example and human beings are NOT simplistic. ALSO, the child who grows up in this example, does not necessarily know as an adult that they are operating from what their parent taught them. OKAY?

Now, as an adult they go out into the world, doing nice things for others until one day, they expect not only nice things in return, but usually they attempt to control the other person or persons through emotional guilt and black-mail...GET IT? That is why the title of this Pearl is "*Be Wary of People Bearing Gifts*" because often times, (not always) one can find themselves being controlled by another and emotionally blackmailed.

What can one do? Try to always keep balance in your boundaries, in your giving and receiving. Watch out for those who want to do TOO MUCH, GIVE TOO MUCH...there may be a price to pay that is TOO HIGH!

Remember balance in all things! But then, that is another Pearl!

STICKS AND STONES MAY BREAK MY BONES, BUT NAMES CAN NEVER HURT ME!

WARNING

We all remember growing up with this oldie, but goodie! As adults, we know differently. In this day and age of bullying both in person and through social media, names and words can hurt us AND hurt us very much! I would like to focus on how words can hurt.

Children learn from their parents, adults and peers. If all adults paid closer attention to how we use words to convey our thoughts and feelings, maybe our children would learn better ways of approaching difficult situations with others.

Let me give an example…

Often when I work with couples, the language they use with each other is what I call "commentary language". This language sounds like snide sarcasm with resentment and degrading comments. The goal being to make their partner feel less than, disrespected, and to hurt them. Often times, they are put in a position to have to defend themselves from the tirade being hurled at them. The reason why I call it "commentary language" is because it is based in comments and opinions that are meant to inflame a situation or the other person. Now, I ask you, is that any way to treat someone you love? Does it get you what you want?

When asking couples those two questions, the usual responses are, "I hadn't thought of it that way and no, it doesn't get me what I want".

My feedback...I understand at the time, it probably feels REALLY GOOD to berate someone, tear them down, and "word vomit" all over them. However, a kind, loving, decent human being would not treat people that way.

When a person behaves in this despicable way it is your ego talking! You must be feeling not important enough, not understood enough, not loved enough, not ____________ (fill in the blank) enough (all uncomfortable feelings)...for that is what ego does! It protects us from our uncomfortable feelings!

Unfortunately, as your tirade continues, ego does not tell the other person what is REALLY going on inside! It is simply annihilating them. This would be called in therapy land, a maladaptive coping mechanism. How do we create an adaptive coping mechanism?

We take a moment, just before we are going to "word vomit" all over our loved one and ask ourselves...SELF, what is really going on with me? How am I really feeling? What is my goal here and how can I use my words to share with this wonderful person how I REALLY FEEL!

Try that...see if it works! Words are very powerful tools to be used to communicate with others! Maybe if we adults learned to use our words like we try to teach our very young children...our children would not grow up bullying and berating others who might simply make them feel uncomfortable (you know, those pesky uncomfortable feelings)!

The next time you are upset, try to remember who you are talking to and find the best words to communicate what you are truly feeling. Then ask for what you want. You may not always get it, but you will feel heard and understood!

Remember...*sticks and stones may break my bones, but names* (words) *can never hurt me!*

A bruise on an arm or leg will heal.* A bruise on the heart, maybe not!

*Just to clarify, I am not suggesting anyone physically hurt another. I am simply metaphorically describing this chapter's title.

BIRDS OF A FEATHER FLOCK TOGETHER

SUGGESTION

I remember when my mother said this to me when I was a teenager. She meant it was important for me to cultivate relationships with people who thought the same way I did, wanted the same things I wanted, had the same morals and ethics.

Recently I was working with a client whom I have known for many years now. She stepped back into session for what I call a "brief tuneup". I will call her JR (her initials)!

A bit of background....JR has been working very hard for the past several years towards a career. Careers take time, energy and money...the three finite resources we humans have to spend on self and other. After struggling to get her career off the ground, JR was finding success and prosperity. Things were good!

One session, JR and I were discussing dating and friendships. Navigating both can be time consuming and tricky. Especially with a successful career that needed looking after daily.

We were discussing boundaries (remember what I preach, RTL - respect, trust, love for self first and then other) within the genre of finding a significant other and navigating friends. What JR was discovering was when a person has healthy boundaries for self, prospective partners and friends may drop off and may not be a good fit for you any longer.

All of a sudden in the midst of our talk, JR exclaimed boisterously, "I am an eagle and I am flying with ducks!" We both laughed aloud! Now, let me qualify....there is nothing wrong with ducks! Ducks are beautiful birds, however, if you feel you are an eagle, flying with any other type of bird probably won't work for you! It certainly wasn't working for JR!

You see, JR is a go-getter and a very driven person. Her work ethic and stamina creating a career for herself has tended to leave quite a few both old and new friends in the dust.

It is not JR's job to slow down the momentum of her drive just to be at the same pace as her friends and love interests. It is her job to fly as high as she can go!

So, if you are an eagle, fly with eagles! If you are a duck, fly with ducks! If you are a swan, swim with swans! Whatever analogous bird or animal that speaks to your heart, your drive, your being, go find more of them....

Because, *birds of a feather, flock together* and your success in life will soar!!!!

BREAKING UP IS HARD TO DO

WARNING

Down dooby do down down....
Don't take your love away from me
Don't you leave my heart in misery
If you go then I'll be blue
'Cause breaking up is hard to do!

— BY NEIL SEDAKA

We all know this tune...just a short excerpt from the whole song. You are probably humming it right now in your head. There have been many songs throughout our human history that tell about the "whoas" of breaking up. So, why is it so difficult for us? Haven't we heard enough songs, read enough books, seen enough romantic comedies and tragedies to be able to do it differently? I think not!

First of all, let's examine the phrase *breaking up.* If it is already broken, the relationship I mean, why do we have to break it again? Haven't both parties suffered enough? Clearly, if we are contemplating ending a relationship, why do we have to get to a point where we have to break it to smithereens!

My hypothesis comes from the very saying of this chapter. *Breaking up is hard to do* is not just a saying, it is a doing. It is the end of something once thought of as lovely and precious. A deep connection with another human being where vulnerability lived and our deepest secrets of self were revealed. Recognizing the end of such a heartfelt bond would lead us to try and hold on. To try and make it work until in the end, we have mangled it beyond recognition into something so hurtful and painful. After imploding any shred of what used to be our most treasured relationship, we finally give up, let go and break up! Why do we do this?

Why can't we figure out to "exit stage left" with grace and dignity?

I think we humans are taught from a very young age....quitting is not okay. We better not quit that sport, musical instrument or job. We better not *burn any bridges* behind us! Oooooooh! That's another chapter!

We are taught that if we quit something, if we walk away, we must be losers! So, we hang in there. We hang in there until we hate that sport, that musical instrument, that job and that person we used to care so deeply for at one time. How do we step out without feeling like a "quitter" within any scenario we find ourselves?

We do it with...what do I preach? Respect, trust, love (RTL) for self first, then other. We realize that our younger selves chose what or who we devoted our time and energy to and now our older selves have changed. That's okay! There is no need to beat our younger selves or others up. We knew what we knew, when we knew it, and now, we know something different. That's all! That's it!

In present moment, we have come to a conclusion about our former choices and we wish to end things. Maybe, for a time we hang in there to see if the situation will change. Maybe our view will change. Maybe "they" will change. If after a brief period of time, our view has not changed, so be it. Now, it is up to us to honor our former choices.

Remember we were given free will, the ability to choose and the responsibility for our choices. We need to honor our former choices and our current choices. To not honor our choices means to discount us! Don't do that to yourself!

Once you get to this point, now you will be able to gracefully exit this relationship whatever the scenario (partner, job, sport, music, etc.) with dignity. There will be no need to blow it all to smithereens!

Yes, *breaking up is hard to do*! Even harder and more hurtful without grace and dignity! Remember to hold fast to your RTL!

NOTE: As I write this chapter I want to acknowledge that some uncouplings are more complicated, involve children and many years of being together. I didn't say that walking with your RTL would be easy. Having grace and dignity in what can be a brutally tough emotional journey will not be easy. On the contrary! However, I do believe in RTL and the merit it brings to any situation no matter how difficult. And for those of you who find yourselves in an extremely difficult crossroad, my heartfelt empathy for all you must endure to get to the other side!

BETTER NOT BURN ANY BRIDGES BEHIND YOU

WARNING/SUGGESTION

Here is my mother again!!! I added this chapter because *burning a bridge* is all about some relationship you cultivated with your time and energy. For some reason, the relationship is not working out, you may be really angry and distraught, but there's that old saying from your childhood, *better not burn any bridges behind you*! Yeah!!! I call b*llsh*t!

In some ways, the world has become much smaller. The internet has made it so. We have all been warned that anything put on the internet lives forever and can come back to get you. That may be true, but, I have been in those situations where I have *burned that bridge* and lived to tell about it. Not only that, I *burned that bridge* at a big company and was offered my job back two years later! Why? Because people have short memories, turnovers happen frequently and maybe I had a good reason to do what I did! But let's not make this about me....I have a better example!

Many years ago I worked with a great guy. His name was Randy and he worked in the film and television industry.

Randy came to therapy because he felt he was headed for a nervous breakdown based on his current work environment.

As his story unfolded it became abundantly clear the company had grown exponentially without growing the staff to support the amount of product being produced. Everyone, not just Randy seemed overworked and burned out. Randy's skill set was very marketable, but he was having a hard time even conceptualizing he could get a new job. Why you might be asking? He had been taught he *better not burn any bridge behind him.* He had internalized that early lesson his parents taught him to the detriment of his health and wellbeing.

Once he got passed that early message, he was able to put his resume out there and in a short period of time, he got a new job. This new job had a more reasonable production expectation, better pay and better benefits.

The moral of this chapter….don't wait until your health and wellbeing suffers to a point of detriment because you are worried about *burning a bridge*. Go ahead and burn it! It will be okay. And if you burn it with your grace and dignity intact (RTL) you never know….you could be like me and get asked back. But then like me, maybe going backwards won't be the answer for you!!!

Construct new *bridges*!!!! And *burn* the old ones behind you!

I'VE GOT NO HORSE IN THIS RACE

SUGGESTION

Before I begin, let me qualify this saying! I am NOT talking about horse racing!!!! Like most sayings, this one is metaphorically speaking....okay? Let's move on...

I really like this saying because it tells someone the other person has no investment in the outcome of a particular situation or life scenario. Sometimes one has to make an announcement like *I've got no horse in this race* in order for the other person to realize they are fighting for no reason. The other person is refusing to engage or fight them, metaphorically.

We have all met these people. They get some idea in their head they are in competition with you for "whatever"....you don't even know you are in this competition. Yet, somehow you end up playing some bizarre game with them.

I met Mary in my office one day and among other topics Mary mentioned her friend Lucy. She had noticed whenever the two of them were with other people, Lucy would begin to go into a "weird" competition with Mary. Mary would tell a story about work. Lucy would tell a story that was more colorful, with more details and had a "happier" ending, for instance, praise from her boss. Mary was not sure what to do about Lucy's behavior. What would you do?

Mary and I discussed some options for her regarding Lucy's behavior. One option would be to sit down with Lucy and ask her was she aware of the underlying competition that seemed to be going on? Another option was to not be in the company of others when hanging out with Lucy as it seemed as if Lucy only behaved this way in front of other people. A drastic option would be to end the friendship. Mary wasn't very interested in ending the friendship because she had known Lucy for a very long time, had shared much and truly valued the relationship.

I mentioned this saying to Mary in a session. After a brief discussion, Mary reached a decision. When it was just the two of them, she would tell Lucy, *I've got no horse in this race* perhaps with a bit of humor and a smile which might open up a dialogue between the two of them.

It was hurting Mary's feelings thinking Lucy needed to be in this competition. Mary wanted no part of it and maybe, something else was going on with Lucy. All of this would take much courage on Mary's part!

As it turned out, something was going on with Lucy. She was struggling with a bigger issue and the competitiveness was simply a symptom. Both women talked it out and both felt better afterwards.

If you find yourself in some game you never agreed to play, think about this saying! It could be someone in your life is going through something difficult, doesn't know how to talk about it and doesn't know they are in a *horse race* only with themselves!

On the other hand, you may encounter someone who truly is in a *horse race* with you for reasons unbeknownst to you. If so, do your best to walk in your RTL, allowing them whatever is going on with them to live over there. Does that make sense? Go back and read in Pearls, Book 1, Chapter 26, *Don't catch that ball.* Whatever is going on with them, belongs to them. Not you! Remember *it's not about you!*

IT'S NOT ABOUT YOU!

SUGGESTION

This seems to be a relatively new saying these days, although, my mother used to say something similar to me when I was a child. She used to say, "The world does not revolve around you!" This meant I needed to stop only thinking about myself or I might be behaving selfishly. I have an entire soapbox I could stand on regarding being selfish verses being self-full but that will have to be a video on the YouTube channel!

Anyway, my mother used to tell me that particular saying all the time. We now know all children think the world revolves around them and as children we cause everything. We think we caused the argument, the bad mood, the divorce. It's just not true. Same goes with *it's not about you* when we become adults. Obviously both of these sayings are close cousins of one another!

Here is an example:

We have all encountered someone who is having a bad day. Sometimes that person, even a loved one, can turn their bad day on us. In psychology, that would be termed "displacement". It is important to remember that their bad day does not need to be our bad day. It is our job to realize *it's not about you* and not to take personally their displacement.

We could take care of ourselves by using "I" statements. We could convey to the person their displacement is not appropriate. Especially if it comes from one of our loved ones.

Now, if it comes from the clerk at the market or our boss, we might not want to voice our care of self and simply choose to walk away. OR, we might want to ask, "Is there something I can do for you?" Sometimes, an act of kindness says it all! Only YOU can decide the appropriate course of action given the particular circumstances you find yourself.

I would like to go a bit deeper into this *saying* psychologically...sometimes we humans can get really caught up in making everything about us! Have you ever had one of those days? It feels as if every person we encounter, we offend. We seem to offend every driver on the road. Even our pets are having a hard time with us!!!

Whenever you might have one of those days, take a moment and check in with yourself. Reality check yourself... ask could I really be offending everyone? Probably not! Most likely, you may be feeling a bit vulnerable and sensitive to everyone and everything around you. If after you reality check yourself, you find you have truly not offended anyone, your side of the street is clean, conclude *it's not about you.* At least not how everyone is perceiving you. YOU might need to take a moment to nurture yourself. Ask yourself the question I suggested earlier in this chapter. Ask yourself, "Is there something I can do for me?" Maybe a small act of kindness for yourself is all you need!!!!

THE TRASH TOOK ITSELF OUT

WARNING/SUGGESTION

One of my clients recently said this in session and we both just burst out laughing! I think this saying is a relatively new saying in the world as in the twenty-first century. Having looked it up, it is attributed to a song lyric by Taylor Swift! Go figure!

Many of you who read this one probably already know what it means, however, I have included it in this book about *"Self and Other"* because it says a lot without saying a lot, very simply!

If the *trash has taken itself out* in your life, be grateful! It means you dodged a bullet! Look at me with the multiple metaphors! It means you don't have to take it out. It means that relationship didn't need to happen and you are better off. The sooner it happened, the better!

So, how does *the trash take itself out*? In the case of my client, she drew a boundary line, several of them with a new love interest. He didn't like her new boundary lines. She noticed his behavior change and POOF! He left the relationship by blocking her on all social media!

She breathed a sigh of relief, felt she didn't waste too much time on him and concluded *the trash took itself out*!

Enough said!!!

MUCH ADO ABOUT NOTHING

WARNING/SUGGESTION

I can't tell you how many times I have sat in a room with someone going on and on about nothing. They could literally discuss the exact color of the sky that day, how many different kinds of birds they saw that morning, or recite the "precious" trick their dog performed yesterday.

The problem is this person tells the same stories over and over again including more detail with every passing moment not realizing usually they are over embellishing and making a big fuss about the most mundane of subjects. This is a person who is guilty of making *much ado about nothing!*

They usually don't see the affect they are having on the people around them due to being so involved in the particulars of the story they are telling. It is as if they are in their own world of them!

Could this be a form of narcissism? What do you think? The jury is out for me. I think because most people who are going on and on about nothing are trying to fill a void, sound more interesting and look more engaged in the conversation. In other words, I don't think they are "holding court" to purposefully harm anyone or to make themselves the center of attention. I just don't think they are aware they are doing it.

So if this is to be a "warning"...my question to you the reader, do you behave in this way? If so, what are you willing to do about it?

Another form of this behavior might be someone who suffers from anxiety. Without going into diagnoses, this issue can be very debilitating for a person. Unlike the person previously mentioned, the person who suffers from anxiety, can't help it. It is as if they spread anxiety like "peanut butter" across all thoughts and life situations which can cause them much upset.

So what does one do with a friend or loved one like this? Here are some "suggestions"...

You could go in one of two directions. The first direction would be to sit down and ask them if they are aware of their behavior. This may come as a complete surprise to them. They may also become upset with you.

The second direction would be to accept them for who they are which would inform you of your behavior and what you are willing to do within that acceptance.

NOTE: Let me go one step further and give a short psych lesson on the difference between *content* and *process*. The first person I mentioned who seems to go on and on speaks in *content* meaning many words and phrases. The second person I mentioned also seems to go on and on with much detail in every story they tell. Neither one of them ever talks about their feelings on the topics they are describing. If they did, they would be talking in *process*.

For example: The first person in this chapter describing all the birds they see in their yard every morning. Instead of describing each bird in depth (content driven) they would mention how the birds made them feel, (i.e., happy, content, peaceful) thereby, speaking in process driven language.

The second person in this chapter who suffers from high anxiety is telling every detail of a situation that was upsetting (content), never getting to the feelings they felt (process) while experiencing that situation. Does all of this make sense?

I think this is the best I can do on this chapter. After all, I never want to be thought of as a person who goes on and on and spouts *much ado about nothing!*

Next!!!!

KNOW YOUR AUDIENCE

SUGGESTION/WARNING

Right on the heels of *much ado about nothing* comes the chapter *know your audience!* As one shares with others, please take into account to whom you are speaking, allowing both yourself and other to have a meaningful exchange of ideas and conversation.

Let's give an example:

As a practicing psychotherapist it is my job to assist clients in their growth or whatever propelled them into therapy meaning *I join them where they are in their journey.* It is important for me to not talk over their heads. I have been steeped like a teabag in the jargon of psychology for many years. My clients not necessarily. So, it is important I speak to them from a space of knowledge with explanations and concepts they can grasp and understand. Frequently, I will check in with a client to make sure they get what I am describing to them because what good does my knowledge do if my client can't understand and put what they are learning into practice in their life? Therefore, I *know my audience!*

Here is another example:

Recently at a dinner party, one of the guests showed my husband a book about guitar playing. There had been conversation around the room about music and playing an instrument, mainly the guitar. My husband plays the guitar. The gentleman who handed my husband the book was an admitted novice guitar student. He started to tell my husband all about the book, what he was learning and that maybe my husband could get that book, thereby, learn from it as well.

Now, my husband is a kind man. He took a moment and looked at the book out of kindness, then handed it back to the gentleman. He never told the man he was speaking to that he has a Master's degree in music with an emphasis in classical guitar. The man never asked one question to my husband about his guitar playing. Knowing nothing about my husband, he automatically assumed they were on the same page and the same level! He was not practicing *know your audience!*

Later that same evening, the gentleman began telling me about serotonin and dopamine and how they work in the brain. Having asked nothing about me all evening, he assumed I knew nothing about these two neurotransmitters. Imagine if he had known he was speaking to a licensed psychotherapist! But he never asked.

Can you see how important it might be to *know your audience.* On so many levels we connect with others every day. We have opportunities to learn about other people which enhances our lives, making our lives richer and fuller!

So take a moment to *know your audience!* Your life will be better for it!

PATIENCE IS A VIRTUE

SUGGESTION

Hmmmm! You might be thinking....this chapter should have been in the first book on *"Self"* and you would be correct! I could have written it for *Book 1* as I often suggest to clients to have patience for themselves, as well as, others. So, I will combine the two for this book, *"Self and Other" Book 2.*

Whenever you lose your patience with a person or situation have you ever noticed if you take a moment to reflect, often times you are as upset with yourself? Some of you reading this right now are probably saying, "H*ll no! Never!" I contend if you truly take a moment within that upset, you will feel anger towards yourself. You may even inwardly berate yourself for dropping the ball, not paying attention, not following through...the list of self recriminations can be endless.

I say STOP! RIGHT NOW! KNOCK IT OFF! Why?

You are not being patient with yourself or the other person. You are not being kind to yourself or other. You see, kindness creates patience!

The meaning of kindness is being gentle and caring.

Patience is a virtue! The meaning of patience is the acceptance of trouble, delay, or suffering without upset. The meaning of virtue is behavior showing high moral standards.

So...if we approach others with gentle caring (kindness), acceptance of trouble along the way, maybe with some delay (patience), striving for behavior that exhibits high moral standards (virtue) we have achieved a monumental goal!

BUT, this begins at home! Within ourselves! We must first give ourselves kindness and patience to develop that virtue before we can give it to others.

As always an example:

John and Molly were what I would describe as a "power couple". They seemed to have it all. Successful careers, three great kids, a beautiful home, family and friends. So, what brought them to my office?

Molly began by telling me lately tempers seemed to be very short between the two of them. Depending on the situation at hand, if one of them dropped a ball regarding a chore or task, the other would become very angry and upset. They could feel themselves drifting apart and never seemed to have a nice word for the other. Neither one of them understood what was going on only that they couldn't seem to communicate with one another anymore. They both wanted to fix things, but didn't seem to know how.

After asking many questions of them both, I began to see the issue. Within their *family system* much energy was being expended in many different directions. Their careers were on fire, both very successful with a lot of attention and focus. The kids were involved in extracurricular activities which also took focus.

Molly and John both admitted to me most of the time they felt very spent. Sometimes, house chores didn't get done, appointments were missed (i.e., dentist, dog groomer). They admitted they had a lot on their plates.

I asked both of them how angry did they get at themselves when something didn't get done? Both confessed very angry. I asked how angry do they get at one another when something didn't get done? Again, both confessed very angry. Here's what I told them…

I commended them for being so successful and high functioning. I acknowledged they had a lot going on in their lives. I warned them about "burn out" and conveyed genuine concern for them.

Then I told them what my therapist told me many years ago when my husband and I were in a similar scenario.

I posited I believed they were experiencing a "zero battery charge". Neither one of them had anything to give the other. Whenever each tried to "get a charge" or lean on the other, there was nothing to give. This resonated with them.

I mentioned my ideology of *patience is a virtue!* I explained to them the ideology of respect (R), trust (T) and love (L) for self first, then other. I wove the thread of RTL in relation to *kindness for self, then other. Patience for self, then other!*

I asked when was the last time either of them was kind to themselves? Had they practiced any self care recently? As you can guess, the answer was no. They had been working so hard they forgot to take care of themselves in a way that nurtured each of them as individuals.

We worked together for awhile putting practical real world tools in place with the goal of self care to recreate the kindness and patience they once had for themselves, then other. This took some practice, as I always say, to create those little and large shifts. This was a hard shift for both of them because they were so comfortable doing for others… job, kids, family, friends. Focusing on self and self care was very foreign to Molly and John. They had to learn to give themselves permission to do things that were just for them as individuals (i.e., hobbies).

Some people spend their whole lives never having a hobby or an interest that "feeds" them! This is an important concept to nurture and it is not selfish!!! It is being kind to you!!!

Patience is a virtue, but it begins with kindness! Remember to be kind with yourself, so you can be kind with others. Remember to be patient with self, so you can be patient with others!

THE SINCEREST FORM OF FLATTERY IS TO COPY*

SUGGESTION

I love this saying! As human beings we are constantly comparing ourselves to one another. Usually those comparisons end up hurting us, others or both. I always warn clients to be careful not to compare themselves to others because there will always be a winner and a loser. Who wants that outcome?

I subscribe to the art of "copy"! After all, we begin copying from the moment we are born. Babies begin by copying and mirroring their caregivers' facial expressions. If a caregiver smiles or sticks their tongue out enough times, a baby will begin to smile or stick their tongue out in response. Why do babies do this? In part because if a baby can get its caregiver to emotionally invest in them it raises the level of success the baby will survive, therefore our species. It is a basic instinct!

As we grow and develop as human beings, we are encouraged to copy others. This is part of our socialization. It is built into us both through nature (being human) and nurture (our environment and people around us).

If we did not have these basic instincts and socialization in our society, we would not have survived. The expression, "no man is an island" is really true. Without the fostering of togetherness I would imagine most species would perish.

Back to copying…it seems a natural, almost instinctual thing we do. As with all ideas I present, balance would be the key. What do I mean?

At the same time we are being socialized and copying one another, we are developing our sense of selves. This takes many years to develop what is called a "solid sense of self".

A solid sense of self is where all parts of our personality (i.e., narcissism, histrionic, avoidant, dependent, borderline, etc.) are less in flux, are more fluid, more seamless and are in balance. In balance means there is no one part of our personality dominating us, creating an imbalance and issue.

When a person has developed a solid sense of self, around 30 years of age or so, they may copy someone, but not lose themselves in copying everyone. Does that make sense? When a person does not have a solid sense of self, they copy everything, constantly. They seem to flit from one notion or idea, easily influenced by everyone around them all the time. This can become very confusing for them. Seeking some help with developing their solid sense of self might be a good idea.

However, if there is something about another person you admire and genuinely like about them and it is within your power to copy it, then go for it!!!! It will never be exactly like them because they are them and you are you! You learn about yourself, your likes and dislikes, your moral and ethical codes, what you stand for, thereby, assisting you in creating your solid sense of self!

Enjoy growing by copying! After all, *the sincerest form of flattery is to copy*!

*"Imitation is the sincerest form of flattery that mediocrity can pay to greatness".

— OSCAR WILDE

I WILL BEAT MYSELF UP MORE THAN YOU EVER COULD

WARNING/SUGGESTION

HA! I just heard this saying on a television show I was watching! I have been saying this for years! It makes me so happy when I hear what is obviously a saying that has become a common thread amongst we humans to the point it is being written into scripts for mass consumption!!! Yay!!!

This is a fantastic ideology to internalize into your being. Both for self and other! Here is why…

When we humans walk with integrity and we do something be it consciously (on purpose) or subconsciously (accidental) and we get it wrong, we will beat ourselves up pretty badly. It has been my experience both personally and professionally….when a human being gets mad at themselves it is way worse than whenever they are mad at someone else. They will beat the ever-loving crap out of themselves. Why? Integrity! So why would you need anyone else beating you up?

Conversely, you can turn that around and recognize your other (significant other, friend, family member, colleague) if they are a human being with integrity will probably do the same when they do something wrong. So, give it to them! Allow them the room and space to beat themselves up for doing something wrong and here is the important message….you ready?

Give them the ***grace*** you would expect from them if the shoe were on the other foot!

Right? Right!!!!

How does that work with verbiage?…."I don't have to beat you up, you are gonna beat yourself up enough."

One last thing…

Don't beat yourself up too badly. Please! Don't allow someone you love or care for to beat themselves up too badly. Toxic shame will be the result and can lead to tragedy. We all make mistakes. We all have lessons to learn and no one said those lessons were easy or cheap!

The next time you or someone you love messes up, remember to hold yourself in *warm regard and don't beat yourself too badly.* Remember to hold the other person in *warm regard and allow them the grace.* Remind them to hold themselves in *warm regard.*

Oh wait! Warm regard is grace! Without grace we would not learn from our mistakes! Our mistakes is how we learn our lessons!!!!

THAT FISH WAS THIS BIG! EXAGGERATION

WARNING

Exaggeration means to represent (something) as being larger, better, or worse than it really is. Everyone exaggerates! I would like to think people exaggerate to make a point. By punctuating a story with exaggeration, the person listening to the story understands the magnitude of the storyteller's experience.

Unfortunately, for some people, exaggeration becomes a habit. The sad truth is the person who allows exaggeration to become a habit has no clue the effect their over embellishment has on others or themselves. Exaggerate too much and one can lose family and friends because this person can no longer be respected or trusted. What do I preach? Respect (R), Trust (T), Love (L) for self first, then other. The person who exaggerates is not respecting, trusting or loving themselves enough, so they cannot exhibit RTL for others either.

Here is my humble opinion and hypothesis...originally, these people exaggerated often because they never felt as if they were enough. Now, many years later, they are firmly entrenched in an exaggeration habit and have no idea they are doing it. It has become of way of life for them.

As we know, habit forming behaviors can be known as addictions. When I was researching the topic for this chapter I came across many quotes about exaggeration.

This one stuck out for me...

"There are some people so addicted to exaggeration that they can't tell the truth without lying!"

Have you ever met someone whose exaggerations are so frequent, you catch them lying? I have met such people. They wreak havoc in the lives of others to the point people will cut them off and never speak to them again. At the very least, the people they are able to keep in their lives never believe a word they say, so meaningful conversations and true interactions for them are lost. It is a very sad state of affairs!

In the extreme, as I have been discussing, the person who habitually exaggerates has no idea their "storytelling" isn't real. They believe what they are saying with such conviction it leaves one wondering if they have lost their mind. At the very least, the ability to monitor what comes from their mouth is non-existent. Consequently, they are perceived as compulsive, pathological liars. Compulsive meaning they can't help themselves. Pathological meaning their exaggerations have become a mental illness. Do you think they can change?

In psychology, one gets 50% credit for having awareness of their behavior. The other 50% is earned by figuring out what they want to do about their behavior and then putting newly learned tools into practice towards change. A person who can't help themselves and has a mental illness probably lacks the self awareness and agency to make any change towards stopping habitual exaggeration.

Let's look at an example:

Jack says he holds a license in general contracting. No one has ever seen his license. Jack is a very charming, nice man who sounds like he knows what he is doing. He gets hired often. But Jack has a problem no one knows about...He over exaggerates his abilities and skills all the time when talking with potential clients. Even with the clients who have hired him, he over exaggerated his skill level. His razzle-dazzle stories regarding past jobs, how beautiful the jobs were and how happy his clients have been with his work seemed to work with people.

This "double talk" or "word salad" spun people out. Often, his over exaggerations confused people, sometimes making them feel intimidated by him, resulting in not wanting to ask too many questions. Sometimes while on a job, Jack would talk for so long that valuable time would be eaten up and the client was paying for that time. After awhile, clients avoided Jack as they didn't have the time or the extra money to listen to him.

This created many problems for Jack's clients because the jobs were often completed late and sometimes in a subpar manner. The state of these jobs caused an assortment of issues including fire hazards, falling hazards, rain hazards, etc. You get my drift!

Jack had no idea how he was coming across to others! There is an expression...*he is a legend in his own mind.* He was so busy touting his knowledge and abilities, he didn't see the damage he was doing to himself, his reputation and to others. Often times, when he finished a job, he walked away with no idea how unhappy his clients were with his work. Clients had learned not to engage him in a discussion because they knew it would get them nothing but more exaggeration and storytelling. Often times, they would cut their losses to get Jack as far away from them as possible. They would end up hiring another contractor to redo part or all of the job Jack botched. They chalked it up as a "lesson learned" and moved on. Jack would move on to his next client and the process would start all over again.

As I mentioned this is an extreme example. Let's discuss a couple of less extreme examples and the more common forms of exaggeration…

When someone uses dramatic or absolute language for example: Dramatic: *"I'm* ***freezing to death****, I am* ***so hungry*** *I could* ***eat a horse****, I feel* ***so sick****, I* ***wanna die.*** Absolute: *You* ***always*** *behave that way, I* ***never*** *act like that,* ***everyone*** *thinks you're a* ***terrible*** *person,* ***no one*** *likes you".*

Dramatic language is an exaggeration used to drive a point home and usually doesn't hurt someone. Absolute language is an exaggeration used to manipulate or harm someone, even you!

How? Absolute language will often negate your point and/or not allow someone to truly understand what might be going on with you. I will not focus on dramatic language because it is fairly benign in it's consequences.

Let me see if I can conjure up an example of absolute language…

Jimmy says to his mother, "You ***always*** yell at me, you are ***always*** mad at me. I can ***never*** do anything right!" His mom, Nancy had just gotten frustrated with him because she asked him numerous times to clean his room that week and he hadn't gotten around to it. She did raise her voice to him in frustration, however, most of the time, Nancy tries her best to be reasonable with Jimmy. She learned in therapy yelling at Jimmy simply makes her the bad guy, then he doesn't have to take responsibility for anything because Mom is being mean.

The truth of it is, Jimmy did forget to clean his room after agreeing to several times during that week. But, with good reason! He was studying for finals, had two end of season soccer games and with all that studying and practice, he simply forgot! By using absolute language, he negated the very REAL reasons he had for not cleaning his room and he looked like a victim. If he had explained to his Mom what happened that week, she probably would have helped him clean his room. Another lesson she learned in therapy, but that's another chapter called *Landscaping* and is in *Pearls Book 3, the Parenting book*!

And here is an example of using absolute language that hurts others:

Whenever a person uses absolute language to manipulate another person, they are using it to hurt them. They manipulate them into thinking they must be "all bad or all good". Using verbiage like "***No one** likes you. **Everyone** thinks you're a weirdo*!" Get it?

Who is the "no one" or the "everyone" in this example? Could that really be true? If the person on the receiving end of this kind of manipulative, dare I say, bullying technique can take a moment to challenge those statements...they would probably conclude that "some" people like them just fine which means the absolute language being used is not true.

In conclusion....be careful how often you exaggerate! You could be setting yourself up like Jack to not be believed. Or like Jimmy, to negate an honest struggle you are in, thereby, not allowing another person to understand you. Or you could just be a bully trying to toxically shame another person! In any of these instances, your relationships with self and others will suffer!

Enough said!

NOTE: The truth is we are all a "mixed bag" of positives and negatives giving us balance within ourselves and hopefully we can look at others with the same balance. Try to examine situations with the same balanced view. And don't forget to *consider the source* of who is using absolute language and why!

CONSIDER THE SOURCE

WARNING/SUGGESTION

Often times when we are in a conversation with someone, we are concerned with how they are perceiving us. We never think about how we are perceiving them. Oh sure, sometimes we will make judgments about others usually when we are feeling threatened in our egos. How dare someone judge us! But rarely do we take a moment to step back and truly *consider the source.*

Let's check out this example:

I was working with Matt one day and he was really having a tough time trying to remember what a good guy he was. Matt had been my client for about a year. He was one of those lovely people who takes on too much responsibility when in relationship with others. He was always willing to take the blame if a conversation went awry between himself and a friend.

In one session quite a while ago, Matt was sharing he had really upset his friend, Emory. He felt he had let his friend down. I reminded him again he only gets 50% of the responsibility of a relationship, his friend gets the other 50. This was always a hard pill for Matt to swallow. He had begun to accept only 50%, but once in awhile, he would backslide. That day, he was backsliding.

Here is how the story unfolded. Some time ago in a conversation between the two friends, Matt had asked Emory about his childhood. Emory had confided in Matt some important details about losing his first pet, a dog named Ray. At the time of the conversation, both Matt and Emory grew closer as friends, deepening their bond by sharing some poignant stories about their childhoods.

Matt has spoken about Emory many times during sessions. He holds Emory in very high regard. Emory was one of his closest friends. It is good to have close friends.

Sometimes when Matt spoke of Emory, I got the feeling Emory was a very precise, detail oriented kind of guy. Not much got past Emory. Whereas, Matt has admitted on more than one occasion, details seem to fall through the cracks with him. I have reassured him we are all not created the same and wouldn't the world be a boring place if we were all clones of one another? Usually, he saw my point.

As I mentioned earlier in this story, he was really upset with himself. He told me the other day when talking with Emory, he forgot who Ray was when Emory mentioned him. This upset Emory a lot. Emory became very mad at Matt, even going so far as to threaten to never tell Matt anything important about himself or his life.

I asked Matt to tell me again the narrative of when he and Emory had exchanged those heartfelt stories of their childhoods. How long ago was that? Matt answered, it had been over a year. I asked, and when you both were in the middle of those stories was empathy present? Did each of you walk away from that exchange feeling cared for and respected? Matt answered yes, then went into berating himself for screwing up and was now examining all of his friendships and wondering if he dropped the ball similarly with other friends.

I let him go on for a few minutes until he caught his breath. I asked him, would it be presumptuous of me if I made an assumption about Emory? Matt said go ahead…I asked him if Emory was a very precise, detail oriented guy? He said yes. I asked was Emory really good at remembering things? Matt said yes. Then I said, well *consider the source.*

I explained to Matt we all have certain gifts and cool things about us. Emory has a precise, detailed gift that allows him to remember things others might not. Matt has different gifts like how steady a person he was, which could be very comforting to someone.

Emory wasn't looking at his friend, Matt. He was projecting who he was onto Matt expecting him to remember the details of a conversation had a year ago.

Matt was forgetting who Emory was in that moment. If he had *considered the source* the conversation might have gone very differently. He could have told Emory he remembered he had lost his beloved dog, how it felt to hear the story, how much he missed his first pet.

I understood Emory's upset. Just not to the level of anger he went to with Matt. Emory was not *considering the source* when viewing Matt, needing to remember their friendship and their different strengths they bring to the table.

The next time you are in a conversation with a friend remember when they say something that might offend, might seem ignorant, might seem weird…ask them, what did they mean by that? Get curious and open up a dialogue and always remember to *consider the source!*

I LOVE YOU TO THE MOON AND BACK! DOES UNCONDITIONAL LOVE EXIST?

SUGGESTION

Often, I have asked my clients this "challenge question"...*does unconditional love exist?*

People usually take a moment to answer. There is no right or wrong answer. This is an open discussion about conditional vs. unconditional love. Here is my critical thinking answer...

I believe the closer you bring someone to you (see the video on my YouTube channel called *Shiny Penny*) the more conditional love becomes. Think about it! The people we expect the most from are those we bring in the closest to us. I expect a lot from my husband. I think he expects a lot from me. Some examples would be: moral and ethical views (very serious) to whether both of us keep a clean house (a bit less serious, still important and can be learned). Does that make our love conditional? You bet it does!

Let's look at unconditional love. At the end of this chapter, you will read a quote from Martin Luther King, Jr. I think he sums up unconditional love very well, which is why I chose it. Within his quote he combines unconditional love with acceptance. The key word here being acceptance.

Unconditional love is the acceptance of them/of other. That is the gift! But, what if in accepting them for exactly who they are, results in you getting hurt? Is that okay?

I believe unconditional love exists, however, you must put some conditions on yourself. Confused? In order for us to love someone unconditionally, we have to decide how close to bring this person into our lives in order for them not to hurt us. We can accept them for who they are, appreciate them for being them (we are all a mixed bag of stuff) and keep them "at arms length" from us, thereby, avoiding any hurt they may cause us. Make sense?

Let me expand a bit more on this even though I think these concepts of conditional and unconditional love are pretty clear.

We bring people into our lives, especially our significant others so they will "push" our "unfinished business" buttons (usually from our childhoods) and challenge us to change. It is important both people in this significant relationship figure out how to rise to those changes. This is conditional! And it should be, if you are planning to spend the rest of your life with this person.

NOTE: Seeking professional assistance as a couple to help both of you figure out how to shift some of those "unfinished business" buttons will help you grow through them.

Conversely, if you have a friend or family member who is "weighted" in never changing...Whose values, morals and ethics are very different from yours, but they have some things about them you love and appreciate....then unconditionally love and accept them. How? By keeping them at a safe distance from you so their way of being and behaviors can't hurt you.

I love you to the moon and back is a lovely sentiment meant to convey how much one person loves another. It does not constitute license to unconditionally love someone that is harmful.

Next!

> "The greatest gift that you can give to others is the gift of unconditional love and acceptance."
>
> — MARTIN LUTHER KING, JR.

FAMILIARITY BREEDS CONTEMPT WHILST ABSENCE MAKES THE HEART GROW FONDER

SUGGESTION

Here is another oldie but goodie! What is interesting to me is how many times I will say this to clients in a session reminding them when they spend too long with family and/or friends *contempt* will rear it's ugly head. When spending time away from family and/or friends *fondness* returns and we miss the ones we love.

The suggestion of this chapter is to remind yourself when heading into a scenario involving those you love with a plan for an extended stay *familiarity will breed contempt* at some point, so be prepared. Remember in psychology one gets 50% credit for having the knowledge, so acknowledging the possibility of this outcome will help you to shift accordingly. The other 50% is what are you willing to do to thwart the situation you may be in to avoid the *contempt*. Let's explore some possibilities because I know how tough it can be to draw a boundary line with well meaning parents, friends or other family members you may be visiting…

My mother (yep here she is again) used to always tell me to "never overstay my welcome". Wise words! If you find yourself on an extended stay with loved ones make sure you plan some day trips or even some overnight trips to different parts of the country you are visiting. This gives everyone some room to breathe in-between hanging out. It goes without saying, but I will say it anyway....please be a good houseguest! Make your bed, clean up after yourself in the bathroom, offer to do the dishes after a meal. Many adult children will go home to visit parents and become the children they were when young....don't do that!!!! Be a responsible adult! Your parents will thank you for it and be impressed with you. They will respect and trust you more (oh, there's my ideology again, RTL).

Another idea to avoid that nasty *contempt* is to stay nearby in a hotel or motel. Now, that may be harder than it sounds... let's look at a real life example.

Anita was a successful businesswoman in the Los Angeles area who originally hailed from Texas. Every year she and her son would visit her sister and stay at her house. Her sister didn't really have room for them, but made due with an inflatable mattress in the den. They shared a bathroom with her sister's children. Needless to say, it was a bit crowded, but family is family and they were all together under one roof.

Anita was getting ready to plan their yearly visit, but as she was learning healthier boundaries in therapy, she was having some second thoughts about staying with her sister. She acknowledged in prior years when she left her sister's house there were hints of resentment on both sides of the family.

We discussed all the possibilities and I watched as my client struggled with the idea of not staying at her sister's house. Staying nearby at a hotel brought on some anxiety for all the obvious reasons...the money, what if her sister felt hurt, what if the family were insulted. Then we looked at the alternatives...more space for everyone, not sharing a bathroom except with her son, having the ability to leave when needed to create some "air" and "respite" for family to breathe.

When trying on both of those dresses (*See Pearls, Book 1*), Anita could feel in her body how much more relaxed she was at the prospect of the hotel stay vs. the tightness she felt at staying with her sister again. Her decision was made.

Now, all she had to do was tell her sister. She was dreading the prospect and rightly so. When drawing new and unfamiliar boundaries with others, especially loved ones, we are usually fearful of their response. We never want to hurt anyone's feelings.

It took courage on Anita's part to have that conversation with her sister. She knew it was the right choice for all of them. And guess what? Her sister took the news very well. No issues whatsoever! Anita was pleasantly surprised. When she returned to session after her trip, she reported it was one of the best visits had by all. She told me she thought maybe her sister was feeling the same strain. By drawing the healthy boundary, Anita felt she had taken care of everyone in a good way.

That is what healthy boundaries do…they take care of you and the other person simultaneously. Everyone wins!!!

So remember…*familiarity breeds contempt, whilst absence makes the heart grow fonder!*

Act accordingly!

THE GREATEST GIFT YOU HAVE TO GIVE ANYONE IS YOURSELF! DON'T GIVE IT LIGHTLY!

SUGGESTION/WARNING

I tell people this all the time! I love this saying! Not many people truly know how valuable they are and how important it is for someone in their life to earn the gift of them.

I think this concept has to be learned. Just like whether love is conditional or unconditional, giving yourself to another person has conditions. Period!

I have said before and will say again, we have three (3) finite resources to spend in our lives. Time, energy and money! None of us is living a three hundred (300) year lifetime, so when we spend time with someone, we are giving them a gift of our time, as they are us! We only have so much energy to expend in a day. When we spend our energy with another person, that is a gift of our energy, their energy as well! My mother used to say, "money doesn't grow on trees!" Of course not, so if we spend money on someone it is a gift, as it might be spent on us as well!

It is important for exchanges between people to have balance! Have you ever walked away from someone feeling drained? Know why? You spent too much energy and they did not reciprocate with the same amount of energy in return. This exchange was not balanced. Please make a note of the imbalance for next time, if there is a next time and act accordingly.

Beyond these substantive constructs of time, energy and money lie the very real and valuable concepts of self. Kindness, warmth, the ability to be genuine and vulnerable, to be real with others…these are the gifts I am addressing as most important! Maybe you can think of a few more because of who you are and what you bring to your relationships!

Since everyone likes examples, here goes…

Every time Jeremy sees Paul he knows he is "in for a pound, not for a penny". This is a great saying for another time, but for this example I am stealing it.

Jeremy has known Paul since middle school. As long as they have been friends, Paul has a habit of getting Jeremy into situations that cost Jeremy dearly.

One time, Paul asked Jeremy to go on a trip with him. They were flying to Vegas for the weekend. Paul had his plane ticket, but unbeknownst to Jeremy, that is all Paul had. They got to Vegas and you guessed it, Jeremy had to pay for the room, the food and even the gambling! To top it off, Paul got seriously drunk in the hotel bar, insulted the bartender, tried to pick a fight with him and almost got kicked out of the hotel. At the end of this latest Paul adventure, Jeremy was exhausted. He went to work the next day not feeling or looking his best and it was noticed. Now, Jeremy is a very nice person, cares about Paul, however, sometimes it's just too much! When he has tried to discuss how he feels with Paul, Paul waves him off, quickly changes the subject, so Jeremy never gets to advocate for himself. This pattern of their friendship began long ago in their youth, but both men are adults now in their early 30's. It might have been okay when they were younger before they had greater responsibilities. As adults the stakes are much higher and Jeremy isn't sure what to do with Paul.

Does he end this friendship? Does he limit his exposure to Paul (see the *Unconditional Love, Chapter 24*)? Does he try and talk to Paul again?

Jeremy struggled with what choice to make many times. It was clear to him something needed to change. As he discussed it with me in several sessions, *trying on each pair of pants* (see *Pearls Book 1*) he came to understand he was giving too much value to this relationship and to Paul with little reciprocation. Paul didn't seem to value Jeremy the same way Jeremy valued him. What do I always say, "balance in all things". There was a major imbalance happening here.

In the end, Jeremy chose to *unconditionally love* Paul by moving him a bit away. By not having him in so close (see *The Circles* video on my YouTube channel) he could continue to have Paul as a friend. By not allowing him to wrangle Jeremy into some cockamamie (now, I am showing my age), crazy adventure costing him his time, energy and money. I applauded him for the decision he made to draw healthy boundaries based on respect (R), trust (T) and love (L) for self (Jeremy) first, then other (Paul).

You see how complicated being in relationships with "others" can become? What would you have done?

GASLIGHTING

WARNING

Gaslighting gets a lot of attention these days. Having an awareness of whether someone is gaslighting you is pretty important! *Gaslighting* is a form of psychological abuse, is manipulative and downright nasty!

Gaslighting comes in many forms. Projection is one of those forms. Projecting their actions onto you, for example, accusing you of a wrongdoing when the accuser is the one who committed the wrongdoing in the first place.

Denial and making you feel crazy are two forms of gaslighting. Your partner is cheating on you. You confront them. Your partner denies it, and makes you feel as if you are crazy for thinking they are a cheater.

Gaslighters make you believe you are incompetent or play on the people and things you love. They will play separation/splitting games with you to get you to hate your job (something you care for), think you are a bad parent (your children you love) or that your friends (people you trust) are against you, whittling you down until you question everything and everyone.

Eventually, the person being gaslit no longer recognizes

themselves in the mirror. They have become so dependent on the gaslighter (which is the goal) they are a shadow of their former selves. Their confidence, backbone and surety of their world has been shattered.

I have worked with a few people in my practice who were victims of gaslighting. They wanted so much to believe their partner had their best interests at heart. As their stories unfolded in my office, it was clear to me they were being manipulated and controlled. How was I to help them?

I began with full transparency about my suspicions this person was not looking out for their best interests. I would give examples from their stories of what was suspect. They listened, however, it was very difficult for them to believe this person they loved could be this sinister.

I explained a hypothesis around this loved one. This partner had learned to operate this way in the world long before they met my client. This was a coping mechanism typically learned in childhood for them and they were probably unaware of how they behaved towards others. I shared with my clients, most likely, this behavior was not about them, but about their "other". The one (other) they loved!

I would ask them to tell me what they were like before they met this person. What were their prior relationships like and how were they within those relationships?

Within those narratives, I found the pieces of them that used to be before this damaging person came on the scene. I found their strengths, their love, their heart, their joy, and their wholeness. I helped them build back who they were before this person came into their lives.

Typically, I got much resistance from these folks. You know why? Because they would have never behaved this way towards someone, so it was hard for them to think someone would behave that way towards them. That someone they loved who loved them would not have their best interests at heart!

I get it! Most of us have met people who gaslight! I have had a few of these in my past. Both significant others and friends. My empathy for my clients as they struggled with the reality of their loved ones not being healthy for them was based in my own past and struggles. I had to admit those folks were not good for me. It took a minute! I did my best to help my clients understand their partner, their friend wasn't good for them either.

The last exercise I would suggest was…I asked my clients to write down and make a list whenever they felt suspect of their partner's motivations, if they had any behaviors or words that confirmed their suspicions. I asked they please bring it in with them for discussion.

The clients who completed the exercise began to see concretely what their partner was doing. This is akin to building a case against them where the proof is right in front of you. My clients could no longer deny or make excuses for their partner. They had begun to understand what they were experiencing at the hands of this "other". Some of them left their partner. This is very brave and takes a lot of guts! Often times, people have to take a minute to rebuild themselves into the strong person they once were before that relationship in order to end it.

One more thing about people who gaslight! When you draw healthy boundaries with them to take care of you, they will eventually leave you. Why? They can't control you anymore. Here is a real world example…

Patty came to my office seeking therapy to try and figure out how her three (3) year relationship had gone off the rails. She was so confused. She had been understanding and patient for much of their relationship as Ken (her significant other) worked towards separation from his spouse so he and Patty could finally be together.

A bit of history....Patty and Ken had met one another when both of them were married. Patty knew her marriage was over, as did Ken or so he said. They began an affair. Shortly after the affair began, Patty left her husband, filing for divorce. As we know, divorces can be difficult and painful for all parties involved. Patty's divorce was no exception. Eventually, everything was finalized and Patty was able to move forward with plans to be with Ken. But, here she was three (3) years later and Ken still hadn't left his wife. Patty chose to come to therapy to try and figure it out.

As I mentioned earlier in this chapter, as Patty was telling me about the past three (3) years, I began to suspect Ken of being a gaslighter, as well as, some other possibilities. He accused Patty of cheating on him. Meanwhile, he was still married. He accused Patty of not loving him and not really wanting a relationship with him. Meanwhile, Patty completed her divorce and was free and clear to have a healthy relationship.

I encouraged Patty to describe to me who she was before she met Ken. What was her marriage like to her ex? What about relationships before her marriage? What was she like as a friend? The picture of Patty I got was someone who was kind, fair, warm, objective, loving, moral and ethical. In other words a balanced human being. The Patty who came to my office that first session was not balanced and was questioning her very thoughts and behaviors.

After a bit of therapy, Patty began to come back to herself. She began to believe what I was telling her as I poked holes in Ken's behaviors and stories. Once in awhile she would fall back into disbelief he could be this sinister or dastardly, which would be normal for anyone to do.

One session, Patty shared with me she thought Ken had

been stringing her along. I suggested she draw a boundary with Ken in the form of an ultimatum. Therapists don't typically suggest ultimatums as a way of approaching someone because they are very black and white and the person making the ultimatum will have to follow through with it or lose credibility. So I knew this might be a gamble.

I put forth to Patty she tell Ken she is tired of waiting for him to leave his wife, enough is enough. She has decided she is going to begin dating through a website dating app OR he can leave his wife and they can move forward with their relationship. Patty chose to take me up on my suggestion as she wanted to take back control over her life.

Guess what happened...Ken invited Patty out for her birthday a week later. He told her he had met someone else and their relationship was over. He never mentioned one word about his wife. He accused her of losing faith in him and he simply couldn't tolerate being with someone who had so little faith in him or their relationship. Can you imagine?! After three (3) years! Seriously?!

By drawing a healthy boundary with the idea of self advocacy for Patty, she found out in one week exactly who Ken was. Did you get all that *gaslighting* he was doing? Wow! And you know what, Patty got it, too!

We worked together for awhile longer just to solidify her solid sense of self before she stepped out into the world of dating as she wanted to make sure she would not meet another Ken!

Be careful out there! The next chapter is a guideline I used from the time I was 17 years old. Maybe it will work for you as well!

THREE STRIKES AND YOU'RE OUT!

SUGGESTION

In psychology, if a behavior is repeated three (3) times or more, it is considered a pattern. We therapists look for healthy and unhealthy patterns in our clients. The healthy patterns we support, the unhealthy patterns we help our clients to change or shift.

I knew none of this psychology when I adopted this ideology around 17 years old. I decided if someone in my life exhibited the same behaviors three (3) times or more chances are they would continue to repeat those behaviors. If those behaviors were detrimental to me or my relationship with them, then I would end the relationship.

Three strikes and you're out became one of my mantras. Every boyfriend knew I lived by this mantra. It has served me well over the years mainly because it gave me a guideline for myself to follow. It gave me a boundary allowing me to self advocate.

I have imparted this particular boundary philosophy on many of my clients. Especially the teens and twenty-somethings I have had the honor to work with through the years. A lot of us struggle with "where are our boundaries" when we are young (see my YouTube channel for the video *Boundaries and You*) and how do we develop healthy ones. I love guidelines and this saying is a good guide!

An example of this boundary follows…it is a rather benign or of lesser importance than other boundaries, but I think it will suffice to illustrate my point…

Jim is a great guy! He works hard and has a great group of friends. He feels he is fairly balanced in his life. He has a girlfriend, Janie. Recently, they moved in together. They are in their mid 20's and are hoping this is the one! Someday, in the not too distant future, they will get married, have children and live happily ever after.

After living together for a few months, Jim began to notice a pattern of behavior from Janie. Janie loved to hang with her friends on Friday nights after work. Every Friday night, not just once in awhile. Meanwhile, the laundry built up, the housework built up, everyday living chores were not getting done. I am not saying this is all because Janie went out on Friday nights with her friends, however, a pattern was emerging. Nothing seemed to get handled during the weekends. Janie was just too tired on Saturday and besides, wasn't Sunday supposed to be a day of rest before the work week started again?

Jim sat down with Janie and had a "benign over wine" conversation (see my YouTube channel and the video *Benign Over Wine*). To explain it to the reader, it is a conversation when things are calm, everyone is in a good space so the outcome of the conversation will be successful. I will give this metaphor to many of my clients as it is a good starting point towards having a meaningful conversation with someone you love when both of you are open and available.

I digressed….Jim talked to Janie about how often she went out, how things were not getting done and the household chores seemed to all fall on him. Janie apologized and said she would "course correct" and start helping Jim around the house. They both walked away from that conversation feeling better.

Janie did follow through with her "course correction" for about two weeks. Then, everything went right back to the way it had been before their conversation. Jim accommodated Janie's behavior for a bit, mentioning every now and again their agreement, but Janie would just placate him (*Ego Defenses*, another video on my YouTube channel) to get him to be quiet.

Jim was beginning to see a pattern. He sat down with Janie twice more to have additional conversations with her that included not only the original thoughts about keeping up the household chores, but about spending quality time together as a couple and maybe saving money towards their future. Janie would tell Jim what he wanted to hear, then turn around and do exactly what she wanted with no thought to the agreements they had made.

After the third conversation, Jim knew he had to think long and hard about whether he wanted to continue a relationship with Janie. He loved her very much, but she did not seem as if she wanted the same things he did.

Jim came to therapy to figure out if he was doing something wrong. After a few sessions and finding out that Janie was doing more behaviors behind his back that seemed irresponsible, Jim came to the conclusion…Janie seemed to have a pattern of irresponsible behaviors. He admitted he had seen this pattern when they were dating, but thought once they moved in together, Janie would take their relationship and life more seriously. Unfortunately, that wasn't the case.

Jim ended his relationship with Janie. He helped her move in with one of her girlfriends.

As Jim and I wrapped up our sessions I shared with him my 17 year old philosophy of *three strikes and you're out!* He admitted maybe if he had known that philosophy when he met Janie, he would have ended it much sooner. He was going to carry that philosophy going forward into his next relationship, thereby, holding that healthy boundary for himself, allowing whomever he sought out a relationship with to hold that for herself as well. Maybe between the both of them they would be able to correct patterns of behaviors with each other before they ended up broken up.

And they all lived happily ever after! If it were only that simple! Oh wait! It can be! Keep reading and for goodness sake, go find my YouTube channel!!!

NO GOOD DEED GOES UNPUNISHED
THE ROAD TO HELL IS PAVED WITH GOOD INTENTIONS

WARNING

I have combined these two notable sayings because they say the same thing. Why might you ask? Here we go...

I cannot tell you how many times I or someone I know has tried to do something nice for someone only to have the actions taken backfire or somehow go awry in the worst possible way. This leaves myself or the other someone I know feeling horrible at the botched outcome of my or their very sincere attempt at helping another person. As I sit here writing this chapter I am trying to think of a real world example I can share with you, the reader....I am a bit perplexed. I think it is because most good deeds and good intentions are done without thought of consequences or outcomes. I think they are inspired within the moment of truly wanting to help someone. Someone loved and cared for or simply someone in need. Hence, the punishment or hell one endures afterwards when it all goes wrong. It wasn't thought out. It wasn't done with informed intention. It was a simple knee-jerk response to another's struggle. I wonder if most of our "helping" moments aren't because we have compassion and empathy for another and want to make it better if we can. But do we?

What do we do when we see someone going through a difficult time? Do we help? How do we help? Did they ask for our help? Are we inspired to help them because watching them struggle increases our own anxiety and we want to alleviate our own uncomfortable feelings?

These are all important questions to ask yourself before you volunteer to help someone. The next time you witness someone struggling in their life, remember *no good deed goes unpunished and the road to hell is paved with good intentions!*

Why not start the conversation with, "What can I do for you?" OR "Is there anything I can do for you?" By giving your someone the room to share how you can help, you are showing them respect and honoring their self agency within their struggle.

If they answer one of the two questions above with ways you could help, they will give you the boundaries within you may assist, thereby, honoring both of you in your friendship.

Enough said!

IMPORTANT TO HAVE PEOPLE AHEAD OF YOU THAT INSPIRE YOU AND PEOPLE BEHIND YOU THAT YOU INSPIRE

SUGGESTION

People like this concept! It gives all of us the chance to be in balance and you know what this therapist preaches beyond respect, trust and love (RTL) for self first and then other! I preach balance in all things!!!!!

As the title of this last chapter says it is *important to have people ahead of you that inspire you and people behind you that you inspire!*

If it is alright with you, the reader I am going to use myself as an example....

When I chose to go back to school to study psychology I had two people in front of me that I aspired to be more like....my therapist, Corie for obvious reasons and my husband Robb. Both Corie and Robb had achieved Masters degrees and both were thriving in their professions. I wanted what they had.

As I began college at the ripe old age of 41, it became clear to me there were many young people I could also inspire along my path, so I did! As my life has continued I have done my very best to have people ahead of me that inspire me and people behind me I inspire.

This creates balance but also creates something else. Can you guess what that might be?

If we only had those "in front" of us, we might begin to feel less than. As if we are not good enough for those that inspire. The opposite is true in that if we only had those we were inspiring, we might feel as if we are more than everyone else. Neither less or more than is a good space to live in. One is shaming, the other grandiose. Extremes of a sort and not healthy.

By having those in front and those behind we live in the middle, in the balance as I have said. Being in balance is living in health!

We don't always get to have people in front of us and people behind. It takes a little effort to see those people and appreciate them for the roles they play in our lives.

As you finish this book…try and find those "others" to inspire you and those "others" you can inspire. Life is much more interesting in so many ways if you open yourself up to all the possibilities it has to offer and challenge yourself to grow!

ACKNOWLEDGMENTS

In these times of derision and division, it is more important than ever, we remember our shared realities and that we are not far apart from one another. We are all human and as I remind my clients regularly...we have threads of humanity connecting us. These threads allow us to not feel alone in our triumphs and struggles and to remember "we are all in this together".

Once again, I find myself in the fortunate position of being able to acknowledge some of the most courageous people who inspired me to write *Pearls of Wisdom, Book Two*. In this book, I acknowledged we are not alone, we have each other and our shared reality.

Using my endearing nicknames (you all know who you are), here are some of those peeps I call "others"....

The Dynamic Duo (Handsome Kinesiologist's parents) who worked tirelessly to understand themselves, thereby, achieving the ability to understand one another, deepening their respect, trust and love in the process. No small feat for them!

Techie Boy and the beauty he married chose to free

himself from childhood influences, thus allowing him the ability to open his eyes and see that he chose wisely in his partner. Both are complementary and symmetrical to one another. It makes me smile every time I think of them because they are perfect for one another!

Techie Dad (yup they are related) who found his way inspired by his son's bravery to step out of the shadows of a very busy life working towards a work/life balance that included finding his voice and strength, valuing himself enough for love. Took a moment to convince him how much he was worth! He knows now!

Young Restauranteur….the youngest I have ever met! Intelligent and sweet with the biggest heart imaginable. Wise beyond his years….challenges himself to always see the positive in every situation. This is a gift he brings to everyone he meets!

Trailer Boy as in movie trailers…goodness gracious! KISS…keep it simple sweetheart! That brain of yours keeps you busy. From one over thinker to another…simple is the key!!! Don't spend as many years as I did figuring that out!

Special EFX Guy…I could see your "easy" way of being sometimes wreaked havoc for you with others as they underestimated your strength. They didn't realize your ease was a gift of grace and not to be taken advantage of. With time and practice you began to assert yourself combining your ease and strength not to be trifled with and people felt it!

Physics Boy and Softball Girl…(yup, siblings)! What you both have achieved in your young lives thus far takes my breath away! WOW! What a joy you both have been to those around you! Always remember your value!

The Beautiful Ones, you honored me by embracing all that I had to offer. By putting into practice immediately the lessons I shared, you grew quickly, honoring your choice of other with truth and transparency. A testament to your respect, trust and love for self first, then one another!

Strong, Exotic Teacher! The strength you possessed to put yourself through school while being a single parent, only to face a bigger challenge in your life, overcome it and learn to accept it makes you one of the bravest people I have ever known. Brava!

Sacramento Girlie!!! I still am not sure why you step into session with me…you are so together, battling challenges both emotional and physical that would put someone else horizontal to the world, and yet, there you are…upright with this sunshine brightness that baffles me. I feel very fortunate to know you as you remind me by just shifting our view we can make a difference in our lives!

Sweet Lady (a contemporary of mine!). Oh my! The immense body of work you have done on yourself through the years is impressive!!!! Writing a book!!! How incredible you are and what a gem!

Precious Family and Delicate Girl…assisting you all through a most devastating turn of life events proved to me how indomitable and resilient we human beings can be when faced with unspeakable sorrow and pain. As I write this, tears come to my eyes and my heart understands why!

I have had the honor and privilege to work with the most incredible "others" these many years and I continue to be inspired by all of them! Thank you for your integrity!

www.ingramcontent.com/pod-product-compliance
Lightning Source LLC
LaVergne TN
LVHW022211200926
848481LV00006B/1930
* 9 7 9 8 2 9 5 5 3 5 2 0 8 *